CHAPTER
ONE

ABOUT
US

The Beginning

First Name: _____

Last Name: _____

Maiden Name: _____

Born (loc'n): _____ Year: _____

Parents: _____

Interesting story about my family: _____

_____

_____

_____

_____

&

First Name: _____

Last Name: _____

Born (loc'n): _____ Year: _____

Parents: _____

Interesting story about my family: _____

_____

_____

_____

_____

THE EARLY YEARS
GETTING TO KNOW EACH OTHER

WEDDING BELLS

Married -
Loc'n Town: _____
Loc'n Church: _____
Officiated:_____ Year: _____
Interesting story about our marriage or relationship: _____
_____
_____
_____
_____
_____

FIRST HOME

Location: _____
Interesting stories about our first home: _____
_____
_____
_____
_____
_____
_____
_____
_____
_____
_____
_____
_____

FIRST JOBS

Loc'n Town: _____

Company: _____

Position: _____ Year: _____

My Boss: _____

Interesting stories about my first jobs before marriage and
after: _____

_____

_____

_____

_____

_____

Loc'n Town: _____

Company: _____

Position: _____ Year: _____

My Boss: _____

Interesting stories about my first jobs before marriage and
after: _____

_____

_____

_____

_____

_____

LIFE TOGETHER
STARTING OUR LIVES TOGETHER

CHAPTER
TWO

ABOUT
US

Family

CHILDREN

First Born: _____

Born On (Date): _____Time: _____

Born In (Town):_____ Year: _____

Weight: _____

Interesting stories about _____'s birth:_____

_____

_____

_____

_____

_____

_____

Second Child: _____

Born On (Date): _____Time: _____

Born In (Town):_____ Year: _____

Weight: _____

Interesting stories about _____'s birth:_____

_____

_____

_____

_____

_____

_____

CHILDREN

Third Child: _____

Born On (Date): _____Time: _____

Born In (Town):_____ Year: _____

Weight: _____

Interesting stories about _____'s birth:_____

_____

_____

_____

_____

_____

_____

Fourth Child: _____

Born On (Date): _____Time: _____

Born In (Town):_____ Year: _____

Weight: _____

Interesting stories about _____'s birth:_____

_____

_____

_____

_____

_____

_____

CHILDREN

Fifth Child: _____

Born On (Date): _____Time: _____

Born In (Town):_____ Year: _____

Weight: _____

Interesting stories about _____'s birth:_____

_____

_____

_____

_____

_____

_____

Sixth Child: _____

Born On (Date): _____Time: _____

Born In (Town):_____ Year: _____

Weight: _____

Interesting stories about _____'s birth:_____

_____

_____

_____

_____

_____

_____

FAMILY
MEMORIES OF A YOUNG FAMILY

FAMILY
CAREER CHANGES

FAMILY
GROWING CHILDREN

FAMILY
TEENAGERS

FAMILY
YOUNG ADULTS

CHAPTER
THREE

ABOUT
US

Empty Nest

EMPTY NEST

GETTING TO KNOW EACH OTHER ALL OVER AGAIN

EMPTY NEST

HOBBIES AND INTERESTS

CHAPTER FOUR

ABOUT US

Our Family Grows

MARRIAGES AND GRANDCHILDREN

Couple:_____

Married (Date): _____

Loc'n Town: _____

Loc'n Church: _____

Officiated:_____ Year: _____

Interesting story about the wedding or the relationship:

_____

_____

_____

_____

_____

_____

Couple:_____

Married (Date): _____

Loc'n Town: _____

Loc'n Church: _____

Officiated:_____ Year: _____

Interesting story about the wedding or the relationship:

_____

_____

_____

_____

_____

_____

MARRIAGES

Couple:_____

Married (Date): _____

Loc'n Town: _____

Loc'n Church: _____

Officiated:_____ Year: _____

Interesting story about the wedding or the relationship:

_____

_____

_____

_____

_____

_____

Couple:_____

Married (Date): _____

Loc'n Town: _____

Loc'n Church: _____

Officiated:_____ Year: _____

Interesting story about the wedding or the relationship:

_____

_____

_____

_____

_____

_____

MARRIAGES

Couple:_____

Married (Date): _____

Loc'n Town: _____

Loc'n Church: _____

Officiated:_____ Year: _____

Interesting story about the wedding or the relationship:

_____

_____

_____

_____

_____

_____

Couple:_____

Married (Date): _____

Loc'n Town: _____

Loc'n Church: _____

Officiated:_____ Year: _____

Interesting story about the wedding or the relationship:

_____

_____

_____

_____

_____

_____

MARRIAGES

Couple:_____

Married (Date): _____

Loc'n Town: _____

Loc'n Church: _____

Officiated:_____ Year: _____

Interesting story about the wedding or the relationship:

_____

_____

_____

_____

_____

_____

Couple:_____

Married (Date): _____

Loc'n Town: _____

Loc'n Church: _____

Officiated:_____ Year: _____

Interesting story about the wedding or the relationship:

_____

_____

_____

_____

_____

_____

GRANDCHILDREN

First Grandchild: _____

Parents: _____

Born On (Date): _____Time: _____

Born In (Town):_____ Year: _____

Weight: _____

Interesting stories about _____'s birth:_____

_____

_____

_____

_____

_____

_____

Second Grandchild: _____

Parents: _____

Born On (Date): _____Time: _____

Born In (Town):_____ Year: _____

Weight: _____

Interesting stories about _____'s birth:_____

_____

_____

_____

_____

_____

_____

GRANDCHILDREN

Third Grandchild: _____

Parents: _____

Born On (Date): _____Time: _____

Born In (Town):_____ Year: _____

Weight: _____

Interesting stories about _____'s birth:_____

_____

_____

_____

_____

_____

_____

Fourth Grandchild: _____

Parents: _____

Born On (Date): _____Time: _____

Born In (Town):_____ Year: _____

Weight: _____

Interesting stories about _____'s birth:_____

_____

_____

_____

_____

_____

_____

GRANDCHILDREN

Fifth Grandchild: _____

Parents: _____

Born On (Date): _____Time: _____

Born In (Town):_____ Year: _____

Weight: _____

Interesting stories about _____'s birth:_____

_____

_____

_____

_____

_____

_____

Sixth Grandchild: _____

Parents: _____

Born On (Date): _____Time: _____

Born In (Town):_____ Year: _____

Weight: _____

Interesting stories about _____'s birth:_____

_____

_____

_____

_____

_____

_____

GRANDCHILDREN

Seventh Grandchild: _____

Parents: _____

Born On (Date): _____Time: _____

Born In (Town):_____ Year: _____

Weight: _____

Interesting stories about _____'s birth:_____

_____

_____

_____

_____

_____

_____

Eighth Grandchild: _____

Parents: _____

Born On (Date): _____Time: _____

Born In (Town):_____ Year: _____

Weight: _____

Interesting stories about _____'s birth:_____

_____

_____

_____

_____

_____

_____

GRANDCHILDREN

Ninth Grandchild: _____

Parents: _____

Born On (Date): _____Time: _____

Born In (Town):_____ Year: _____

Weight: _____

Interesting stories about _____'s birth:_____

_____

_____

_____

_____

_____

_____

Tenth Grandchild: _____

Parents: _____

Born On (Date): _____Time: _____

Born In (Town):_____ Year: _____

Weight: _____

Interesting stories about _____'s birth:_____

_____

_____

_____

_____

_____

_____

EMPTY NEST

MARRIAGES AND GRANDCHILDREN

CHAPTER FIVE

ABOUT

US

Twilight

TWILIGHT

FRIENDS LOST

TWILIGHT

MEMORIES

TWILIGHT

LOOKING BACK

TWILIGHT

TOMORROW – LOOKING FORWARD

TWILIGHT

THOUGHTS FOR MY CHILDREN AND GRANDCHILDREN

74667799R00044